**Super H**

# How a Physician Came to Believe in Teachers who are True Super Heroes.

My experiences at the International Conference of the Learning Disabilities Association of America in San Antonio Texas.

ALEXANDRE G. TAVARES

ALEXANDRE G. TAVARES

Copyright © 2013

Alexandre Garcia Tavares

All rights reserved.

ISBN-10:     1493682210
ISBN-13:     978-1493682218

Book cover design by
Shawn Encarnacion
www.shawnsportfolio.com

## CONTENTS

1. Essay: "50th Annual Conference of the Empathy Heroes League: A Success Story" — 1

    Wednesday, February 13, 2013, first day of conference — 1

    Thursday, February 14, 2013, second day of conference — 5

    Friday, February 15, 2013, third day of conference — 9

    Saturday, February 16, 2013, fourth and last day of the conference — 20

    Sunday, February 17, 2013, one day after the end of the conference — 23

    Afterword to the essay "Empathy Heroes League" — 25

2. Empathy Heroes League: Home Training. The Membership is free and the benefits are indescribable! — 26

3. Closing Remarks — 33

4. Acknowledgments — 37

5. Afterword — 39

6. Bibliography — 41

7. About The Author — 47

8. Terms of Use Agreement — 48

The first step is empathy

# CHAPTER 1: ESSAY: "50TH ANNUAL CONFERENCE OF THE EMPATHY HEROES LEAGUE: A SUCCESS STORY"

I suggested to directors of the Learning Disorders Association (LDA) that the name "LDA 50th Annual International Conference" (held February 13–16, 2013) be changed to "50th Annual Conference of the Empathy Heroes League: A Success Story."

I understood that the conference was already over, so any name change would not be reflected in the handouts and printed materials about the conference that were already in distribution. However, I still requested the name change in order to acknowledge the phenomenal empathy observed at the conference. Please follow my reasoning below, and I think you will agree with me.

Let me start by presenting what I learned at "50th Annual Conference of the Empathy Heroes League."

### Wednesday, February 13, 2013, first day of conference

8:00 a.m.:

Keynote Session: "Building on the Past, Looking Toward the Future," by Brock and Fernette Eide. They presented similar ideas to those included in their amazing book *The Dyslexic Advantage*.

I had the pleasure of chatting with the Drs. Eide right after their keynote session, and they autographed my copy. Later that same day, I sent a thank you e-mail to the Drs. Eide.

Main parts of the e-mail I sent to the Drs. Eide on February 13, 2013:

Dear Dr. Brock Eide and Dr. Fernette Eide,

Thanks for having written two amazing books!

I read your books one year ago. They brought me an immense sense of validation, personally and professionally. I have routinely "prescribed" your book *The Dyslexic Advantage* for families to read. The knowledge you share in your books has helped me to greatly improve the care of my patients and avoid a lot of unnecessary suffering. I also routinely "prescribe" Dr. Schultz's book, *Nowhere to Hide*.

Do you remember the name of the Brazilian filmmaker you know? I was amazed to hear Brock tell about this filmmaker who is dyslexic when we chatted this morning. I am far from being a filmmaker, but I have written three film projects over the last three years. None are completed yet, but I have started the filming for two of them. I learned a lot while writing and thinking about films. (Postscript: I think I am a better physician today because of that. I feel that learning about film-making has shed light on a few blind spots of medical education, especially on how to communicate information. The book Scriptwriting for High-Impact Videos: Imaginative approaches to delivering factual information, by John Morley, was amazingly helpful for me in this. I read this book in January of 2010).

Thanks again! I learned a lot reading your books and I learned a little bit more by talking with you today!

Alexandre G. Tavares

10:00 a.m.:

Presentation: "Who Am I? I Have a Learning Disability," by Larry Silver, MD; Charlotte Edwards, PsyD; Connie Parr, APN, CPNP. Dr. Silver could not present due to a loss in the family. Excellent slides! Very empathic presenters.

Alex's plan: contact presenters to request authorization to distribute their slides to teachers and health-care providers in our community.

11:50 a.m.:

Chat with Dr. Schultz. I accidentally met Dr. Schultz today at 11:30 a.m., before our planned meeting at 6:00 p.m. We chatted about books. Dr. Schultz enquired about my work in Manitoba: work setting, team assessment, etc.

Books we talked about:

A) *Ben Behind His Voices: One Family's Journey from the Chaos of Schizophrenia to Hope*, by Randye Kaye.

B) *The Dyslexic Advantage: Unlocking the Hidden Potential of the Dyslexic Brain*, by Brock L. Eide, MD, MA and Fernette F. Eide MD.

C) *Animals in Translation: Using the Mysteries of Autism to Decode Animal Behavior*, by Temple Grandin and Catherine Johnson.

As I indicated, the book *Animals in Translation* is the most interesting book I have ever read. I pointed out that I especially liked the teaching format of *Ben Behind His Voices*, as it alternates story chapters with "chapter guideposts." I also pointed out how strongly the author, Randye Kaye, presents the importance of peer support and psycho-education (both provided in the author's case by NAMI: National Alliance on Mental Illness). Kaye also notes in her book that no mental-health professional had ever mentioned or recommended that she look for support at NAMI. I told Dr. Schultz that his book,

*Nowhere to Hide*, is therefore extremely important in his area as it provides the knowledge that can help parents and professionals better support kids. It can produce effects similar to those experienced by family members of an adult with schizophrenia when they read *Ben Behind His Voices*.

1:00 p.m.:

Presentation: "Stressed Out of Their Minds?" by Jerome Schultz, PhD. Dr. Schultz pointed out that once he understands the reasons for a child's misbehaviour, no child has oppositional defiant disorder. He pointed out that some repetitive learning activities seem to decrease stress in children. His epiphany was: "probably because the children are learning more effectively!" Again, learning in the way that is most effective for a child leads to positive changes in his or her learning experiences.

2:00 p.m.:

Lecture: (use of assistive technology to help child. Main resources for this child: text-to-speech, software for visual maps, inspiration). Tip from Texas teacher (attendee of the presentation—I failed to take note of her name) to me: DVD "How Difficult Can This Be? The F.A.T. City Workshop: Understanding Learning Disabilities", by Rick Lavoie. She gave me this tip following my comment at the mic about a possible idea on how to help adults be more empathic to children's suffering caused by LDs. My idea: start a presentation about LDs and/or ADHA in Portuguese (not the language of the audience). First five min: only spoken Portuguese. Following five min: spoken and written Portuguese together. My point: audience will understand more when presented with synchronized text and speech. The audience will understand the educational advantage of supported listening and will understand that it can be very uncomfortable to be at school if you are being asked to do something that you cannot do. I pointed out my fear that this "simulation" of Dyslexia would scare the audience (adults) and that they would simply leave.

3:30 p.m.:

Presentation: "Digital Storytelling," by Harold Blanco, PhD. Very enthusiastic presenter. Great sense of humour and very positive.

Dr. Blanco's files hosted at:       http://tinyurl.com/13LDA

Dr. Blanco presented:

Most students improved their reading comprehension when they were first presented with a video on the same topic.

5:20 p.m.:

Alex's follow up plan:

Explore further the possibility of "simulating" the experience of having a learning disability by exposing audience to language they do not speak and introducing text-to-speech and visual aids. Purpose: possibly increase empathy for the suffering caused by learning disabilities and/or ADHD.

To simulate the experience of ADHD, could try to present material with background noises low and then high, as children with ADHD are less able to tune out or ignore distracting ambient noise.

## Thursday, February 14, 2013, second day of conference

8:00 a.m.:

Keynote Session: "Technologies of the Future: Where Assistive Meets Mainstream," by Manju Banerjee, PhD. Main point: what has in the past been considered assistive technology for those with disabilities is now increasingly seen to help every learner.

Dr. Banerjee provided the web link for the excellent list of resources "Assistive Technology and Learning Disabilities":

http://www.sc.edu/scatp/documents/ATLearningDisabilities.pdf

1:30 p.m.:

Workshop: "Parenting for Success," by Cherrie Farnette, BS, MA and Jonathan Jones, MS, RN. Amazing slides! Amazing facts presented in "Themes/Attributes of Successful Adults with LD and ADHD." They quoted the Attributes of Successful Adults with LD and ADHD as per Stanford, 1987 and Frostig, 1999.

Presenter Jonathan Jones: Extremely empathic! (As are so many presenters at this conference). Cherrie also did excellent work.

Alex's impression: empathy! Empathy for the kids' experiences! This is what make the LDA conference attendees so special.

I presented to Jonathan my suggestion of adding one slide with recommended readings. I suggested recommending Dr. Carnegie's books, especially *How to Make Friends and Influence People*, and Dr. Kazdin's parenting book. I suggested looking at the nine principles summarized at the end of the abridged version of this book, as these remarkably resemble what the presenters tried to convey today. In my words: strong focus in being empathic to the children's needs and focusing on the strengths of the kids—focus on success, focus on validation.

He suggested taking an advocate/friend to IEP meetings.

Jonathan mentioned the power of positive affirmations during his lecture. After his presentation, I decided to look for quotes from the Roman Emperor Marcus Aurelius' book Meditations.

I sent a thank-you e-mail to Jonathan on the same day.

Copy of the main parts of the e-mail message:

Dear Jonathan and Cherrie,

Thank you for your amazing presentation! Your enthusiasm and empathy were contagious! I never saw a video of Dale Carnegie speaking (probably not many videos available, as he died a while ago), but I have read his books and I thought today that he was probably as empathic as you both were in your presentation!

Here are some books I suggest you consider adding to your presentation as recommended reading to continue the "empathy enrichment" of the attendees of your presentations:

1) *How to Make Friends and Influence People*, by Dale Carnegie. There is also an abridged version of this book. At the end of the abridged version, the main nine principles Dale Carnegie taught are listed. The principles are also available online. Basically, the same ones as you told us today.

2) *The Kazdin Method for Parenting the Oppositional Child*, by Alan Kazdin. The name of the book is misleading. This is a book about positive, solution-focused, empathic parenting. I recommend that every parent read it. After they read this book, the typical phrases I hear from parents at their next appointment with me are, "We (parents and kids) prepared a reward chart together," and, "The nagging at home disappeared!" When I ask kids if they want to continue the reward chart, they answer: "Yes! I like the reward chart." Therefore, this book models the same kind of solution-focused, positive parenting that you and Cherrie explained to us today. This book also clearly presents the concept that parenting programs do not always equal parents imposing their wishes on their kids.

I recently heard a popular parenting book writer (not Dr. Kazdin) state basically, "Parenting programs equal parents imposing their wishes on their children, completely ignoring the feelings of their children, etc."

I imagine this bright and well-intentioned professional came to this extreme view from his frustration of learning about kids' views and wishes being completely ignored in some parenting programs. I see where he is coming from, and I share his frustration, but the methods of Dr. Kazdin are definitely not like this stereotype.

I think the two books above match your presentation completely. I suggest that you remember to mention that the name of Dr. Kazdin's book is misleading. It should be called *How to Develop Collaborating with Your Kids: A Behavioural Plan for the Entire Family Including Rules, Routines, and Focusing on Strengths.* The blurb should say, "Follow our program and you all (parents and kids) will be happier and you will have the time and peace of mind to develop more meaningful connections with your children!" The title would be long. However, it would probably shun the parents that need the book the most—the ones currently focused only on "bad behaviours"—so Dr. Kazdin's title is probably a better title for his book. I bet he thought a lot about it.

It is nice to see that so many of us (at this conference) can be so empathic to the needs of kids and adults with learning disabilities and make a difference in their lives. This is the first time I attended an LDA conference. The level of empathy I see in the attendees and presenters is amazing, and yours is phenomenal!

Thanks again.

I hope I will meet you at other conferences in the future.

Alex

Jonathan thanked me for my feedback and suggestions.

## Friday, February 15, 2013, third day of conference

8:00 a.m.:

Keynote Session: "Celebrating Diversity and Culturally Responsive Teaching," by Vivian Correa. Presenter showed great empathy for the experiences of foreign children.

10:00 a.m.:

"Early Literacy Instruction for Young English Language Learners with Disabilities: The Story of Sapo!" presented by Vivian Correa, PhD, University of North Carolina, Charlotte, NC.

She simulated the experience of being a Spanish-speaking student trying to learn in an English-speaking school. Very interestingly, three attendees left the room during the simulation! That was more than 10 percent of the audience. Once the simulation finished, several members of the audience voiced how uncomfortable the experience was. I pointed out to Vivian that three people left, for unclear reasons, but possibly because they felt scared. She stated that she does this same simulation in college and her students never leave, as they would get a zero otherwise! I pointed out to Vivian that we should think about the fact that kids do not have the option of leaving the classroom. Another attendee then pointed out, "These kids act up at school. They show behaviourally." Being a native speaker of Portuguese, I added that I have contemplated the idea of starting a presentation about learning disorders by speaking only in Portuguese (to an English speaking audience), exactly like she did (in Spanish) today, but I feared that the attendees would just leave the room!

Alex's thought number one:

It was enlightening today to see this does happen; adults seem to run away from the uncomfortable situation! However, kids do not run away because they do not have the option to do that. At times, they do try to run away from school, but they are brought back.

These kids are frequently scared at school due to their learning disabilities, ADHD, or because they do not speak the school language (English).

Unfortunately, what frequently happens once kids are brought back to school is that "consequences" for misbehaviour are administered instead of more attention being given to understanding the child's perspective. That is why books like *Nowhere to Hide*, by Dr. Jerome Schultz are hugely important in correcting this terrible situation: adults not understanding what it is like to live with a learning disorder and/or ADHD and assuming children act up at school due primarily to wilful intention. As I heard repeatedly during this LDA conference, all kids would want to read if they could and if they were given the right resources and an empathic understanding of their learning styles, strengths, and weakness.

Alex's thought number two:

**The stories below are very powerful.**

1) "Kindling a Passion for Reading" (Adapted from the article "Kindling a Passion for Literature")

## Kindling a Passion for Literature

By Gigi Whiteside

I have always loved the feel of a new book in my hand, the crackle of the spine when I open it for the first time, the smell of the freshly printed pages. When digital books and electronic readers first made an appearance, I scoffed. I felt it blasphemous to think that an impersonal electronic device could ever compete with a true artifact, a book. But today, as a veteran English teacher, I am going on record to say I have changed my mind.

I teach high school English in a team-taught setting as well as in a small-group resource class. Both scenarios are specifically designed to address the individual needs of exceptional learners. As a special education teacher, each year brings new students with new challenges. And last year brought my biggest challenge yet.

**Engaging Nonreaders**

I had the opportunity to teach a 15-year-old who was labeled a "nonreader." I'll call this student Bella, after a literary character from her now favorite vampire trilogy. She arrived with a school-issued laptop and software that enabled her to listen as printed text was read aloud. Bella used her technology to read all three vampire novels during the school year. As I witnessed her download and listen to books on her laptop as she read along, I thought, if I could provide the same technology for all of my struggling readers, maybe they would show the same thirst for reading as Bella.

However, Bella was an exception. She was not self-conscious about using the laptop in all of her classes. Two of my other students qualified for computers and reading software but felt conspicuous when encouraged to use them. As I watched these two students refuse their technology, I felt compelled to find a better, less conspicuous, and even "cool" device that could enable them to access printed text.

I began researching various electronic readers, and I settled on the Kindle, a device that had text-to-speech capability. My next step was to find funding. I assembled my proposal, "Kindles for Kids," and submitted it to our PTA. I was thrilled to learn it was approved for a generous grant. I ordered the Kindles, downloaded a few e-books, and watched as the astonishing transformation of my students began.

**Introducing the Kindles**

On Monday, I presented the Kindles to the students. A casual observer would have thought it was a birthday celebration.

The students were ecstatic about trying out the new reading devices. They couldn't wait to download their first books. I was touched to be part of this excitement. Most of these students were reading below grade level. These were the same students who had little interest in selecting from the difficult books at the high school library, who wouldn't consider walking across the street to find easier books from the middle school library, and who had no desire to get public library cards of their own. These were students who complained when informed we were beginning a new novel in class. Rather than the usual, "Do we have to read today?" my students began to ask, "Do we get to read today?"

**Exploring the E-Readers**

The days that followed impressed upon me the importance of evolving toward digital literacy. The first day we had the Kindles, I allowed the students to simply explore their e-readers. My students were quickly able to use the school's wireless internet to download the books they wanted to read. Their exploration turned to mastery within a class period. I wanted their first e-book experience to be positive, so the first semester we practiced reading for enjoyment without the added pressure of a summative assessment. We went online and perused e-books of personal interest. Once they selected their books and obtained parental approval, we downloaded the books onto their Kindles.

In the beginning, I allowed students to read their new e-books only as a reward for completing their classwork. After the first week, they began to request class periods allocated for the sole purpose of reading on the Kindle. My exceptional learners had never "requested" a class period to read quietly before. I was overwhelmed with the high interest these devices brought to my students.

Initially, I did not allow my students to remove the Kindles from the classroom. When I had a student request one from in-school suspension, I caved. He finished his entire book while in detention.

As we approached the semester break, another student begged me to take a Kindle home so he could finish his book. I caved again. This was likely the first time this student had ever wanted to finish a book. He returned the Kindle on Monday unscathed.

## Enjoying the Results

One of the most memorable e-reader moments involved a student who frequently missed class due to discipline infractions and often threatened to drop out of school. One morning I was headed down the hallway, and I heard him yell out, "Hey, Ms. Whiteside, are we reading our Kindles today?" I assured him we were, and he continued, "I was lying awake in bed last night and thinking about what might happen next in my book. Then I thought of something that I was sort of confused about, and I called Bella to ask her, since she had already finished reading it. We talked about the book for a long time." His next comment went right to my core. He said, "You know, I have never looked forward to coming to school, especially staying through to the end of the day. But now, I get kind of excited about reading my book, and I want to be here!"

Even more impressive were the students' passing rates on summative assessments designed to test students' mastery of the state standards. The prior year, my small-group resource class had a collective passing rate of 20%, which was typical for students reading two years below grade level. This year, after seven months with the Kindles, my resource students earned a collective passing rate of 70% on their tests. In my 19 years of teaching exceptional learners, I have never encountered such dramatic results. I am confident the opportunity to use Kindles and the text-to-speech feature positively affected my students' test performance.

Perhaps the best indicator of all is that I have received emails from parents informing me that their children are asking for Kindles as holiday gifts.

## E-Readers Continue to Engage

One fear I had was that the novelty of the Kindles would eventually wear off. I began this year teaching the same group of students. I decided to use the Kindles as the delivery device for my course novels, in addition to the self-selected novels the students would read. Our first e-book was Lord of the Flies, and the students maintained their enthusiasm for using the electronic readers. They have already submitted book requests for me to download, including textbooks in electronic format. The students reported they preferred using Kindles because they were often intimidated by the number of pages or thickness of printed books.

The recent release of the Kindle Fire, which functions as an e-reader and tablet, offers even greater opportunity to engage students with the tools that inspire them. It costs a bit more—twice the price of a Kindle Touch—but offers color illustrations, apps, and the ability to search the web. With e-books, reading becomes fun and engaging. Despite cognitive limits in decoding words and comprehending print, they are able to "listen" to an electronic reader and develop literacy.

Gigi Whiteside, EdS, is an assistive technology specialist for Fulton County, Georgia, USA. She has also taught at Milton High School in Alpharetta, Georgia. She is a member of the Striving Reader Grant Committee, supporting targeted schools through digital literacy.

Reprinted with permission from Learning & Leading with Technology, vol. 39 no. 7, copyright 2012, ISTE (International Society for Technology in Education), www.iste.org. All rights reserved.

And the Story:

2) Story presented in book: Flip Your Classroom: Reach Every Student in Every Class Every Day, by Aaron Sams and Jonathan Bergmann. It is the story of a new English-language learner's family who all (the entire family) started reading the children's books in English once the teacher started providing an iPod with the audio version of the children's books. The family members wanted to read and they could finally read the children's books (with the help of the audio); they were probably learning English at the same time. This is an efficient technique for learning a second language. Therefore, this is a perfect win-win situation. As I have shared with a few teachers at our city, I think this is exactly what most teachers dream: having the entire family reading books with the children at home. Therefore, by using teaching strategies that are empathic to the experiences of the child and their family, we have increased the probability of happiness and success.

A) The students will feel success in their learning – student success in school is an excellent motivator for continued success.

B) Parents will feel success – they will have an opportunity to share in their child's schooling experience (especially with the aid of audio support).

C) Teachers will feel success – their students will be learning more effectively and enthusiastically.

D) The parents will have an opportunity to improve their own English skills.

---

Two paragraphs from Flip Your Classroom: Reach Every Student in Every Class Every Day by Jonathan Bergmann and Aaron Sams. Paragraphs located in pages 30 and 31:

"At conference we attended a few years ago, one of Keynote speakers was a kindergarten teacher who told us this story. She taught in an ethnically diverse school that had many new English-language learners. One of the key ingredients in becoming a good reader is to be read to. She was awarded a grant for some iPod Nanos on which she recorded herself, and others, reading books to her students. They ELL students would then take the iPod Nanos home with the corresponding book and would listen to the story read to them.

As the iPods were continually be used by students she started noticing they were coming back to her with the batteries almost drained. She knew how long the batteries would last and expressed her puzzlement with her students. When parent-teacher conference occurred, one mother told her she was sorry for draining the batteries of the iPod. The mother then told his teacher that not only was she listening to the stories, but so were the grandmother, the aunt, and the whole extended family. The teacher's audio files were educating many more people than she ever expected."

Reprinted with permission from Flip Your Classroom: Reach Every Student in Every Class Every Day by Jonathan Bergmann and Aaron Sams, copyright 2012, ISTE (International Society for Technology in Education), www.iste.org. All rights reserved.

---

I shared both stories above with Dr. Correa following her presentation, I chatted with Dr. Correa for a few minutes. She listened to the story "Kindling a Passion for Reading" with my iPhone app Voice Dream Reader (text-to-speech that highlights the words as they are read) and found it to be an amazing story. I also told her about the second story that I mentioned above, and she also found it to be a very powerful story. I thanked her for her excellent presentation, and I indicated that I did learn a lot from it, especially when I witnessed several attendees leaving during the simulation at the beginning of her presentation. She found this to be an amazing incidental learning experience too. I told her that I have been pleased with the prevailing empathic atmosphere of this conference.

I told Dr. Correa that I was on the phone with my wife yesterday, and I said that it feels like we are all here to develop plans to save the misunderstood kids. As I indicate to Dr. Correa, the word that best describes this conference to me is empathy. She indicated that she was happy to hear my thoughts. I thanked her again and left to attend next presentation at different room.

Related texts available at the Learning Ally website: www.learningally.org

"Tips for Teaching & Learning with Audiobooks"

"Audiobooks will boost grades and improve self esteem"

"Studies Show Audio Textbooks Support Students Learning to Read "

1:00 p.m.:

"Learning Disabilities—Detection, Prevention and Early Intervention," by Mary L. O'Connor Leppert, MD, Physician, Division of Neurology and Developmental Medicine, Kennedy Krieger Institute, Baltimore, MD; Mary Ellen Lewis, EdD, Johns Hopkins University, Baltimore, MD; and Jeffrey Gruen, MD, Professor of Pediatrics (Neonatology) and Genetics, Yale School of Medicine, New Haven, CT.

Alex's notes:

Presenters pointed out that it is frequently hard to connect with families due to many different reasons, such as families which move around a lot, language barriers, etc.

Dr. Mary L. O'Connor Leppert's PowerPoint slides are excellent. She talked about "Issues in Pregnancy that May Result in Learning Disabilities and the Need for Early Identification."

Jeffrey Gruen stressed that nearly 80 percent of variance in reading skills is due to genetic factors.

Answering one attendee's question, Dr. Gruen stated that, although he is not in clinical practice, he is routinely contacted by families who want their children tested. He has observed repeatedly that such families feel validated by a genetic diagnosis. He also stated that these kids with learning disorders are typically quite smart and have other strengths and that he does not see these genetic tests as a way to treat kids but maybe as a way to better plan for the resources these children will need and to guide teachers to the true genetic nature of these disorders.

I then went to the mic and pointed out to Dr. Gruen that, watching his presentation, I feared he would conclude with something like, "So, maybe we will have a cure soon." As I stated, I was very happy to hear his editorial style answer to another attendee's question. I also stated that I see a possibility for increase in the clinical use of genetic testing to bring validation to these children and their families as he has done. What these kids have and the way they learn is very real and is usually not within their control. I forgot to mention to Dr. Gruen (I started presenting the thought, but got sidetracked) that this is the first time that I have attended a conference on learning disabilities and that the empathy that permeates most presentations has been quite evident to me—an empathy for suffering kids who are misunderstood and forced to learn in ways that do not match their learning strengths. I was going to say to Dr. Gruen that I have never witnessed such a level of empathy in any conference I attended before. I also forgot to say that, by helping to bring more awareness to the biological/genetic underpinnings of learning disorders, he is truly helping adults (teachers, parents, family members, health-care professionals) to be more empathic to the experiences of the children. I realize now that, by utilizing his medical knowledge, Dr. Gruen did something similar to what Dr. Jerome Schultz did in his book: Dr. Gruen brought an awareness of what is not readily visible but is still extremely important for us (adults) to understand so that we can better connect with kids.

Alex's note: Dr. Schultz' book is *Nowhere to Hide: Why Kids with ADHD and LD Hate School and What We Can Do About It*. In it, he explains how high stress levels caused by the use of ineffective learning strategies can cause so much stress in children that it may then cause problems with anxiety, school avoidance, and oppositional behaviours. Dr. Schultz did not focus on the genetic causes of learning disorders, but he still brought attention to research on the negative impact of high stress on a child's ability to learn. As he explains in his book, this stress is caused by the mismatch of the learning techniques used and the learning style of the child. Dr. Schultz explains what brain pathways are affected, etc. So he combines neuroscience with real clinical cases in order to help adults be more empathic to different learning requirements of children and to encourage adults to implement the needed adjustments. It was amazing for me to see that even physicians working in basic sciences like Dr. Gruen will still fully exercise this empathic connection with kids whenever given the chance.

Video that can help people understand the biology of empathy: Ted Talk "Paul Zak: Trust, morality—and oxytocin?"

http://www.ted.com/talks/paul_zak_trust_morality_and_oxytocin.html


Alex to do:

A) Ask Dr. Gruen to send a copy of his PowerPoint presentation by e-mail.

B) Send Dr. Gruen complementary copies of two books: The *Dyslexic Advantage*, by Brock L. Eide, MD, MA and Fernette F. Eide, MD and *Animals in Translation*, by Temple Grandin. I decided to order Temple Grandin's book for Dr. Gruen because it is an amazing book about what differentiates the minds of most human beings from the minds of autistic children. The book also presents Temple Grandin's insights on how the minds of animals likely operate. So it is also a book about different kinds of minds, just like *The Dyslexic Advantage*.

## Saturday, February 16, 2013, fourth and last day of the conference

8:30 a.m.:

Presentation: "Empowering the Student with Learning Disabilities in the Elementary School: Self-Advocacy," by Pam Hill, Grande Reserve Elementary School, Yorkville, IL. She provided excellent slides. She was extremely empathic to children's needs. She indicated that she tries to involve kids in the Individualized Education Program (IEP) discussions. She stated that she typically works with kids so they can make presentations at the IEP about how they have been learning and what their learning goals for the next twelve months are. Pam indicated that the kids are typically proud to participate. She helps them prepare to present, review their goals, note progress, and gather evidence of having achieved goals.

She used the phrase, "this is a win-win situation." She stated that involving kids in their IEP discussions and helping them improve their self-efficacy is a "win-win situation." I personally like using the expression "win-win situation."

My suggestions for Pam were:

1) She could consider showing videos of testimonials by kids about their feelings on being involved in their own IEP. (Only after consent is given by both parents and children, of course. The possibility of unintended harm should be carefully explored with the child and parents. For example, is it possible that such exposure will lead to the child being a victim of ridicule?)

2) She could consider inviting kids to present. (Same caveats just mentioned would also apply here.)

This could be extremely powerful, assisting adults in connecting to the true inner experiences of children, and could potentially be a validating experience for the child and his/her family.

Pam welcomed my suggestions. She stated, in fact, that she believes several of her students would love to present at a conference on learning disabilities. I thanked Pam for her amazing presentation and her empathy regarding the learning experiences of children.

I sent an e-mail to Pam a few hours after her presentation.

Copy of e-mail (main parts):

Dear Pam,

Thank you for your amazing presentation today!

I learned a lot! I was happy to watch your sincere enthusiasm for your work with children.

I was happy to learn about your initiative to involve children in their own IEPs.

I wrote the following three words by your slide titled "Plan" (which said, "prepare to present; review goals for progress made; review portfolio for evidence of goals met"):

1) Validation!

2) Education! (Meaning: adults will make every effort to explain to children what they are being involved in and why.)

3) Empathy!

These are the words that came to my mind when I watched your presentation and, specifically, when I heard you present the slide I mentioned.

One question: Did you ever read Dale Carnegie's book *How to Make Friends and Influence People*? If you did not, let me know. I will be happy to send you a copy.

The abridged version of this book has at its end a one-page list of the nine principles he taught. It is a true gem, especially after you read the entire unabridged version of the book. You will probably be amazed to see the similarities between what you have been trying to do and what Dale Carnegie wrote.

I would also like to share that I felt immensely validated to have attended this conference. It was very validating to see that, yes, there are hundreds of people out there that share my personal enthusiasm! I have a lot of enthusiasm for helping adults to relate to the best in each child and for bringing the inner experiences of children to the attention of the adults involved in their lives: parents, teachers, family members, and others.

I found several "empathy superheroes" and countless "heroes" at this conference. I will include you in my list of empathy superheroes at the "LDA 50th Annual International Conference."

## My "empathy superheroes" of the LDA conference are:

A) You (Pam Hill).

B) Dr. Jeffrey Gruen (presented "Genetic Conditions that May Affect Learning"). Dr. Gruen's editorial style comment on how families and children felt validated by knowing the learning disorder was genetically determined—and therefore very real and not the result of limited will as others think at times—was extremely empathetic. So a paediatrician physician doing basic science research is extremely empathic; as he pointed out, such knowledge has the power to validate the experiences of children and adults. Such knowledge therefore helps to eliminate the misunderstandings that we frequently observe when adults do not know that children really learn in different ways not because they wilfully decide, but because their brains are different (not worse).

C) Jonathan Jones and Cherrie Farnette, for their phenomenal enthusiasm and empathy when they presented "Strategies for Developing Success Attributes."

D) Drs. Eide, for their amazing work on increasing the awareness about the advantages not infrequently associated with having learning disorders.

E) Dr. Jerome Schultz, for his phenomenal book *Nowhere to Hide*, as it increases the awareness of readers regarding the suffering frequently associated in trying to force children to learn in ways they cannot. By increasing awareness, he is increasing the chance that readers will be more empathetic to the kids' inner experiences and that the child will learn more and be happy to learn, using the resources he mentions in his phenomenal book.

F) James A. Huff, Learning Disabilities Association of South Dakota, director of outreach. I had the pleasure of chatting with James on two occasions during the conference, and I learned a little about his work. James told me that he has created resources to allow adults that do not have learning disorders to experience how children and adults with such conditions feel at school. This is another effort to help increase empathy for children with learning disorders.

Thanks,

Alex

## Sunday, February 17, 2013, one day after the end of the conference

Copy of the main parts of an e-mail I sent to Jerome Schultz:

Dear Jerry,

It was a pleasure meeting you in person. I greatly enjoyed the chance to talk with you. I think you saw the reason for my previous idea of recording Skype conversations with you; I knew we would have great conversations.

There is still a lot more to talk about. I will take note of the following idea:

Next time we talk in person, I will record our conversation! (If you agree, of course). I think we can produce amazing materials just by transcribing our conversations.

I am currently writing a paper:

"50th Annual Meeting of the Empathy Heroes League"

It is almost ready. I basically just had to collate all that I wrote over the last four days of the LDA conference into one paper. I think now that if I had taken my conference notes directly on Inspiration Software (www.inspiration.com) I would have had the paper ready at the end of the conference! I will try this idea at the next conference I attend. I learned about Inspiration when I read your book (*Nowhere to Hide*) almost one year ago. Thanks! I wrote my conference notes on my Samsung Galaxy Note 10.1. That is the last gadget that I purchased and the one I took to our dinner. I also have two iPads, one iPod touch, one iPhone, one Kindle keyboard, and one PocketBook Touch!

I am writing from home. I arrived here yesterday evening. I attended the conference until 11:00 a.m. yesterday, Saturday, Feb 16, 2013.

I hope you and your wife enjoyed San Antonio.

Thanks for the kind words in your e-mail. We will keep in touch.

Signed,

Alex, "gadget guy" and aspiring filmmaker.

## My conclusion

What best describes the attendees of the "LDA 50th Annual International Conference" is their amazing empathy for the inner experiences of children who have Learning Disorders and/or ADHD. Therefore, although "LDA 50th Annual International Conference" is a literal description of the event, it does not describe what truly happened there. The title I suggested was therefore more accurate for the conference:

"50th Annual Conference of the Empathy Heroes League: A Success Story"

## Afterword to the essay "Empathy Heroes League"

I had the chance to watch DVDs from Richard Lavoie after I left the LDA conference:

- "How Difficult Can This Be? The F.A.T. City Workshop: Understanding Learning Disabilities"

- "Beyond F.A.T. City: A Look Back, A Look Ahead"

- "The Motivation Breakthrough: 6 Secrets to Turning on the Tuned-out Child"

Richard Lavoie's DVDs are excellent resources for every adult trying to develop more meaningful connections with children and other adults.

I wonder if we should have a "Richard Lavoie DVDs watching week" at the beginning of every school year.

Sincerely,

Alexandre G. Tavares, MD, FRCPC
Prairie Mountain Health
Manitoba, Canada

## CHAPTER 2: EMPATHY HEROES LEAGUE: HOME TRAINING. THE MEMBERSHIP IS FREE AND THE BENEFITS ARE INDESCRIBABLE!

### Training Description

In this home training, you will gain the skills to become an Empathy Hero. You can expect phenomenal changes in the way you interact with children: the secret is empathy.

You know who you are. Membership is free and the benefits are indescribable. Become a Super Hero today!

### The Training

I attended the 50th Annual International Conference of Learning Disorders Association in San Antonio and I met amazing people there. I realized the meeting's name was insufficient to describe what takes place at the conference and the type of people that attend. An alternative name for the conference (a name that would acknowledge the phenomenal empathy I observed) is:

"50th Annual Conference of the Empathy Heroes: A Success Story"

I prepared this guide for home training based on this experience.

With this training you will be able to gain the skills necessary to become a member of the "Empathy Heroes League". With these new skills, you can expect phenomenal changes in the way you interact with children: as a parent, as a teacher, as a professional or as a health advocate.

The training will include the following training module topics:

### Training Module 1:

**I will try my best to put myself in children's shoes.**

Activity:

Watch DVD: "The Motivation Breakthrough: 6 Secrets to Turning on the Tuned-out Child"

### Training Module 2:

**I will never know how it really feels to be in a child's shoes. My feet are too big.**

Activity:

Watch DVDs:

A) "How Difficult Can This Be? The F.A.T. City Workshop: Understanding Learning Disabilities"

B) "Beyond F.A.T. City: A Look Back, A Look Ahead"

### Training Module 3:

**I probably don't learn in the same way that children with learning disorders and/or ADHD learn.**

Activity:

Read books:

A) *Nowhere to Hide: Why Kids with ADHD and LD Hate School and What We Can Do About It* by Jerome J. Schultz (Author), Edward M. Hallowell (Foreword)

B) *The Dyslexic Advantage: Unlocking the Hidden Potential of the Dyslexic Brain* by Brock L. Eide M.D. M.A. (Author), Fernette F. Eide M.D. (Author).

C) The *Mislabeled Child: How Understanding Your Child's Unique Learning Style Can Open The Door To Success* by Brock Eide and Fernette Eide

## Training Module 4:

## Children with learning disorders may actually be smarter than me.

Activity 1:

Read Story: Press Release - Glasgow – 16th July 2012 - New Report: Entrepreneurs with Dyslexia Hold Key to Economic Growth

http://www.halfpennydevelopment.co.uk/include/uploads/2012/07/Entrepreneurs%20with%20Dyslexia%20Hold%20Key%20to%20Growth.pdf

Activity 2:

Read Book: *The Dyslexic Advantage: Unlocking the Hidden Potential of the Dyslexic Brain* by Brock L. Eide M.D. M.A. (Author), Fernette F. Eide M.D. (Author).

## Training Module 5:

## We all have different brains.

Are learning disorders the result of a lack of motivation or a different brain structure and different thinking style? Do people choose to have myopia? Children don't choose to have learning disorders. Once children with learning disorders receive their "glasses", they will want to learn; as every child or adult wants to see things clearly.

Activity 1:

Watch DVD: "The Motivation Breakthrough: 6 Secrets to Turning on the Tuned-out Child"

Activity 2:

Reread my notes about the presentation "Learning Disabilities—Detection, Prevention and Early Intervention", included in the chapter 1 of this book.

## Training Module 6:

## Speaking two languages at home is an advantage.

In this module, you will learn skills for teaching in empathetic manner with regards to the needs of foreign families; become an empathy hero with foreign families.

Activity 1:

1. From your public library, borrow a children's book in a foreign language you do not speak. The children's book should have an audiotape / audio CD with the narration of the book.

2. Try to read the book (that is not in your native language) to a child, without the assistance of the audio CD.

3. Now listen to the story with the audiotape / audio CD.

Questions to ask yourself:

- Which way was more effective for you to read the story?
- Which way you learned most?
- Which way was more fun?
- Which way would you like to read other books in a language you do not speak: With or without voice narration?
- If you were a student, which way would you like to learn?

Activity 2:

Read Stories:

- "Bilingual speakers get dementia later in life, Canadian study finds" By Steve Mertl

http://ca.news.yahoo.com/blogs/dailybrew/being-bilingual-may-delay-dementia-canadian-study-finds-171420826.html

- "Speaking a second language may delay dementia" – BBC News

http://www.bbc.co.uk/news/uk-scotland-edinburgh-east-fife-24836837

Activity 3:

Read my notes about the presentation "Early Literacy Instruction for Young English Language Learners with Disabilities: The Story of Sapo!"; included in the chapter 1 of this book.

## Training Module 7:

## The power of validation.

The books *Nowhere to Hide* by Dr. Jerome Schultz and *The Dyslexic Advantage* by Dr. Brock Eide and Dr. Fernette Eide will lead adults with Learning Disorder(s) to feel empowered and advocate even more for children's unheard needs. Validate your children's experiences and become an Empathy Hero for them.

## Training Module 8:

## The secret is empathy.

Activity 1 - Daily:

Read the stories below: Stories with Impact

Activity 2 - Once per week:

Read chapter 1 of this book: Chapter 1: "50th Annual Conference of the Empathy Heroes League: A Success Story"

Activity 3 - Once per year:

Read the book *How to Win Friends and Influence People* by Dale Carnegie

Watch DVDs:

A) "How Difficult Can This Be? The F.A.T. City Workshop: Understanding Learning Disabilities"

B) "Beyond F.A.T. City: A Look Back, A Look Ahead"

C) "The Motivation Breakthrough: 6 Secrets to Turning on the Tuned-out Child"

## Stories with Impact

### We should always focus on success. Look at the best in every child:

- "Essa Academy – An ailing UK school makes an incredible transformation"

http://www.apple.com/ca/education/profiles/essa/

- "Kindling a Passion for Reading"

http://www.amazon.com/gp/feature.html?ie=UTF8&docId=1000816731

- Adapted from the article "Kindling a Passion for Literature"

http://www.iste.org/learn/publications/learning-leading/issues/may-2012/kindling-a-passion-for-literature

- Mild autism has 'selective advantages'

http://www.nbcnews.com/id/7030731/ns/business/t/mild-autismhas-selective-advantages/

- Press Release - Glasgow – 16th July 2012 - New Report: Entrepreneurs with Dyslexia Hold Key to Economic Growth

http://www.halfpennydevelopment.co.uk/include/uploads/2012/07/Entrepreneurs%20with%20Dyslexia%20Hold%20Key%20to%20Growth.pdf

# CHAPTER 3: CLOSING REMARKS

**Correspondence between Donna Davis and Alexandre Tavares – Early May of 2013**

Dear Donna,

I hope you have been doing well.

I am writing to ask authorization to use your video 'Vance's Passion for Helping Others Lives On' at the 2014 international annual meeting of the LDA (Learning Disorders Association).

I had one more idea to submit as a presentation:

'The Amazing Similarities between Patient Centred Care and Child-Centred Learning Strategies: helping you better understand how to best support children in their learning paths'.

I will basically try to compare the ideas from:

1) Your video: 'Vance's Passion for Helping Others Lives On'

2) A clinical case of child who developed severe depression because her learning needs were ignored (I have several true clinical cases that I can merge into one fictitious case)

3) The "On Board model"

4) The idea of empathy being the first step to better connect with a child, as in the essay 'Empathy Heroes League'

Let me know if you approve of me presenting your video at the LDA annual conference as one part of this presentation. I still have to submit the proposal. I made other submissions for presentations but I want to try a few more.

Alex

---

Good morning Alexandre,

By all means you have my permission to use the video at anytime.

Thank you for asking, but please do not feel you have to ask permission to use it (not that I mind knowing how you are advancing patient safety and the patient/family experience). Sometimes I may not get your email in time and I would not want permission to be a barrier to advancing health care improvements. So go ahead and use it anytime, anywhere.

I'm sorry I haven't been as available as I'd like but work and personal commitments, along with PFPSC have kept me very busy. I do apologize and hope all is well with you in your tireless search for patient safety and improvements.

All the best,

Donna

Thanks Donna,

I was happy to read your answer. I can see how we think exactly the same way on such matters: nothing should stop the work to increase the safety of our patients' treatments.

As I joked with Dr. Jerome Schultz in previous email, I think I have a "continuous thinking disorder" (not a real medical disorder), as I cannot stop my thinking. Yesterday, I was in bed trying to sleep and I had the idea of the analogy between patient safety models and the child centred educational models (I do not know if such a term exists) so I woke up to jot down this thought so that I would follow up on it today.

I have another new project. I am putting together essays I wrote into two books. They contain a limited number of pages but I hope they will be very powerful in its impact on its readers. In the first book, "On Board with Your Treatment", I want to include the paper 'On Board' and the movie script 'We AdVANCE'. I hope the movie script will be a powerful text by itself, as it expands further on the reasoning behind the 'On Board model'. The second book will be on Learning Disorders and the role of Empathy. Its backbone will be the essay 'Empathy Heroes League'.

If you ever read the book *The Dyslexic Advantage* by Dr. Eide you will better understand my mind. I still do not know if I can say I have dyslexia, but I strongly feel I am somewhere in that area: this would explain my ability to find 'patterns' in human relations. So, it is like my 'engineer's brain' allows me to analyze human behaviours in a more objective manner. Although this may seam a 'cold way' to connect with people, it is the best way I have found to fill in the gaps for other areas in which I do not excel. So, in the end I am truly warmer to my patients' needs because I can make more sense of their feelings and thoughts and, with this, better empathize with them. My patients often tell me I am very passionate and caring, although I grew up very shy and with a lot of difficulty in trying to find the right words to say things. So, once I overcame these limitations, they no longer held me back, and are today my strengths. This is connected to what I wrote at the introduction of my first book.

Sorry Donna! I got carried away again with inner thoughts and wrote a lot more than I anticipated and now I am hungry too!

Donna, thank you again. I have learned so much in the 6 months of contact we have had so far. You have inspired me.

Thank you.

Alex

---

Dear Reader,

I hope you liked my little book! I tried my best!

If you benefited from the information in this book, please consider sharing a review on Amazon.com. Your recommendation could mean the ideas contained in this book will benefit hundreds of children.

Dr. Alexandre G. Tavares

# ACKNOWLEDGMENTS

I would like to thank all of the people who have believed in me.

My parents and grandparents always believed in my best. My grandparents have left this life, but they are fully alive in my heart. I still remember vividly the sweet words of my grandmothers, always praising the best in me. I don't think they ever complained about my poor attention or made comments on my low language grades in elementary school. I remember my grandmother Gloria saying, "O Xandinho é tão inteligente" (little Alexandre is so intelligent). She was referring to the little engineer Alexandre, who loved to build with blocks and who had creative ideas. My grandmother Celeste valued the role of education and was always proud of little Alexandre too. They believed in me.

I remember my father telling me (at least once a week) that even if he didn't have money for other things, he would give me money for a book (or other study resources). In this way, I could study at home, where I learned best, even when it meant that I would only attend school for a few hours at night. I would start my day by attending a swimming class. This routine would allow me to have my best attention span for the day, and I started to study in the way that was best for me: thirty to forty minutes at a time, with ten- to fifteen-minute breaks for listening to music. I used books, magazines, and videos (I love learning with pictures and graphs). I had piles of educational VHS tapes in my high school years.

My parents never questioned the validity of this style of learning.

My parents still believe in me. Thank you, Dad. Thank you, Mom. Thank you for always believing in me.

Over a year ago, my wife, Renata, said that I should write a book. She was the first to make this suggestion. At that point, I thought, "But there are already so many good books out there, and I don't want to write something that has been written already." One year later, I feel I have come up with something original that deserves to be published. Thank you, Re. Thank you for believing in the best in me, even when I thought I could not do it.

I have to thank two of my most influential teachers: my two sons. They are the ones who have taught me the most about human relations. They have shown me why love should be the guiding thread for all human interactions.

In April of 2012, I read *Nowhere to Hide*, by Dr. Jerome Schultz, and *The Dyslexic Advantage*, by the Drs. Brock L. and Fernette F. Eide. These books brought me an amazing sense of personal and professional validation. It was as if Dr. Schultz and the Drs. Eide had always personally believed in me. I felt a connection with their books. Today, I am lucky to have collaborated with Dr. Jerome (Jerry) Schultz, and we have planned more joint projects for the future. Over the past twelve months, since we first exchanged e-mails after I read his book, Jerry has believed in my ideas and supported my projects. Thank you, Jerry.

I would like to thank my editors, Michael Dietrich and Katie Solbeck, for providing clarity in this book. I would also like to thank all those who have assisted me in reviewing my draft versions.

# AFTERWORD

In my first book, *On Board with Your Treatment! For a Safe Treatment Every Time!*, we examined how being a "trained pilot" (a well informed patient) may be the most important part of treatment and how refusing to make the effort to become informed carries risks that are too high to take.

We also explored how the On Board model, described in the first chapter of the book *On Board with Your Treatment!*, can allow everybody (patients, family members, and health-care providers) to win in the health-care system.

Changing the roles we play in health care may lead to dramatic improvements in safety and avoid an immeasurable amount of suffering for thousands of families, patients, and health-care providers involved in avoidable injuries and deaths that stem from unfair and unrealistic roles. To save lives, we all have to change.

In my daily work, I see that the most important element of an adult who is sensitive to a child's needs is empathy—making every effort to see the world through the child's eyes and believing the best of him or her. But there is a moment in which we realize that it is really impossible to know exactly how it feels to be in a particular child's shoes. We adults are grown, and that does not mean that we are merely a bigger version of the child in front of us; we are all different. So, with this realization, we should move on to the next step: asking.

There is only one way to know how a child thinks and feels, and that is to ask. We must ask children from our hearts, because, when we do that, we open ourselves to an indescribable reward. Fostering empathy in adults toward the inner lives of children and encouraging deeper psychological transformations and personal growth in both the children and the adults who care for them is key.

In February of 2013, I attended "The 50th Annual Meeting of the Learning Disorder Association (USA)." I learned so much that it inspired me to write an essay called "Empathy Heroes League." This is the essay included in this book: *Super Heroes Do Exist!*. I see my experience of attending this conference as a life-changing one by way of validation. Empathy and validation are strongly connected. This is true for any human being.

My epiphany, three months after having written "Empathy Heroes League," is that this same empathy in human relations is a key component in any treatment relationship. The same concepts are strongly connected to my ideas of *On Board*. When we are empathic to a child's inner experiences, we are acting in exactly the same manner as when we are empathic to our patient's treatment needs: we have to hear our patients, they have to actively learn about their treatments, and they have to be at the centre of their treatments. This is the only way to achieve safer treatments and more rewarding experiences for health-care providers.

About the e-mails included in this book: The e-mails were lightly edited for increased clarity and readability. They are being reproduced with the authorization of the authors of the e-mails.

Alexandre Garcia Tavares

# BIBLIOGRAPHY

Note 1:

Of the 46 books below, this writer (Dr. Tavares) read 44 (95% of the books) with either the text-to-speech function of Kindle Keyboard or I listened to the audio version of the book. I only read the paper version of the 2 other books, because these 2 other books were not available electronically (for reading with text-to-speech) and not available as audio books at the time I read them. As of today (December 1, 2013), every book listed below is available with either an audio version or with Kindle version that can be read with a Kindle eBook reader that has text-to-speech.

Note 2:

Most eBook readers do NOT have text-to-speech. This writer owns 4 eBook readers with text-to-speech: one Kindle Keyboard; one Kindle Fire HD, one Pocketbook 912 and one Pocketbook Touch 622. For books in English, my favourite reading device is the Kindle Fire HD. I wish the screen was e-ink and not the LCD screen with back light; as I find the screen of e-ink eBook readers to be gentler with my eyes. For foreign language eBooks, my device of choice is the Pocketbook Touch 622; although I also like to read with the app "Voice Dream" for Apple devices, when the book is not copyright protected, and therefore can be opened with the "Voice Dream" app.

The app "Voice Dream" is my favourite text-to-speech reading app for Apple Devices. For Android Devices, my favourite text-to-speech app is "ezPDF Reader". I do not like to read with the text-to-speech of my Pocketbook 912, as this device generates voice too slowly for my liking.

These are this writer's personal preferences, and may not be the best devices or the best apps existent today or the best device or the best apps for you.

What I want to highlight is that if I did not have my eBook readers with text-to-speech, I would probably only read 11 or 12 books, and not 46 as I did read, due to my slow reading.

## General

*Management Lessons from Mayo Clinic: Inside One of the World's Most Admired Service Organizations*, by Leonard Berry and Kent Seltman

*The Kazdin Method for Parenting the Defiant Child*, by Alan E. Kazdin

*Motivational Interviewing, Second Edition: Preparing People for Change*, by William R. Miller, PhD and Stephen Rollnick, PhD

## Film-making

The book that influenced me the most:

*Scriptwriting for High-Impact Videos: Imaginative approaches to delivering factual information*, Second Edition, by John Morley

Additional books on film-making that influenced me:

*The Power of Film*, by Howard Suber

*The Eye Is Quicker: Film Editing: Making a Good Film Better*, by Richard D. Pepperman

*Film School: How to Watch DVDs and Learn Everything About Filmmaking*, by Richard D. Pepperman and Michael Wiese Productions

## Harvard Negotiation Project and Related Books

*Getting to Yes: Negotiating Agreement Without Giving In*, by Roger Fisher, William L. Ury, and Bruce Patton
*Difficult Conversations: How to Discuss What Matters Most*, by Douglas Stone, Bruce Patton, and Sheila Heen

*Beyond Reason: Using Emotions as You Negotiate*, by Roger Fisher and Daniel Shapiro

*Getting Together: Building Relationships As We Negotiate*, by Roger Fisher and Scott Brown

*Getting It Done*, by Roger Fisher and Alan Sharp

*Getting Past No: Negotiating with Difficult People*, by Roger Fisher and William Ury

## Dale Carnegie and Dale Carnegie Foundation

*How to Win Friends and Influence People*, by Dale Carnegie

*How to Win Friends and Influence People Condensed Version*, by Dale Carnegie

*Comment Se Faire Des Amis (Le Livre de Poche) (French Edition)*, by Dale Carnegie and Didier Weyne (Translator)

*Cómo ganar amigos y influir sobre las personas (Spanish Edition)*, by Dale Carnegie and Roman Jiménez (Translator).

*How to Stop Worrying and Start Living*, by Dale Carnegie

*Dale Carnegie's How To Stop Worrying And Start Living Book Chapter Summary*, by Brian Matthew

*The Quick and Easy Way to Effective Speaking*, by Dale Carnegie

*How to Win Friends and Influence People in the Digital Age*, by Dale Carnegie and Associates

*How to Develop Self-Confidence And Influence People By Public Speaking*, by Dale Carnegie

*The 5 Essential People Skills: How to Assert Yourself, Listen to Others, and Resolve Conflicts*, by Dale Carnegie Training

*The Dale Carnegie Leadership Mastery Course: How To Challenge Yourself and Others To Greatness*, by Dale Carnegie

*The Leader in You*, by Dale Carnegie

*Stand and Deliver: How to Become a Masterful Communicator and Public Speaker*, by Dale Carnegie Training

## Books about Learning Disorders (LDs) and / or Attention Deficit Hyperactivity Disorder

The three books that influenced me the most:

*Nowhere to Hide: Why Kids with ADHD and LD Hate School and What We Can Do About It*, by Jerome J. Schultz

*The Mislabeled Child: How Understanding Your Child's Unique Learning Style Can Open the Door to Success*, by Brock Eide and Fernette Eide

*The Dyslexic Advantage: Unlocking the Hidden Potential of the Dyslexic Brain*, by Brock L. Eide, MD, MA and Fernette F. Eide, MD

Additional books that influenced me:

*Flip Your Classroom: Reach Every Student in Every Class Every Day*, by Jonathan Bergmann and Aaron Sams

*Reading Together: Everything You Need to Know to Raise a Child Who Loves to Read*, by Diane W. Frankenstein

*The Complete Guide to Special Education: Expert Advice on Evaluations, IEPs, and Helping Kids Succeed*, by Linda Wilmshurst and Alan W. Brue

*The Complete IEP Guide: How to Advocate for Your Special Ed Child*, by Lawrence M. Siegel

*Smart Children-Poor Readers: Using Audio/Text-Based Learning for Reading, Comprehension and Language Development*, by Lisa L. Osen

*Driven to Distraction: Recognizing and Coping with Attention Deficit Disorder*, by Edward M. Hallowell and John J. Ratey

*Delivered from Distraction*, by John J. Ratey and Edward M. Hallowell

## Books about Patient Safety

*The Checklist Manifesto: How to Get Things Right*, by Atul Gawande

*Complications: A Surgeon's Notes on an Imperfect Science*, by Atul Gawande

*Better: A Surgeon's Notes on Performance*, by Atul Gawande

*Patient Safety*, by Charles Vincent

## Self-help books and books about Cognitive Behavioral Therapy

*I'm Right, You're Wrong, Now What?: Break the Impasse and Get What You Need*, by Xavier Amador

*Ben Behind His Voices: One Family's Journey from the Chaos of Schizophrenia to Hope*, by Randye Kaye

*Feeling Good: The New Mood Therapy*, by David D. Burns, MD

*When Panic Attacks: The New, Drug-Free Anxiety Therapy That Can Change Your Life*, by David D. Burns, MD

*Cognitive Behavior Therapy, Second Edition: Basics and Beyond*, by Judith S. Beck, PhD

## DVDs

*How Difficult Can This Be? The F.A.T. City Workshop: Understanding Learning Disabilities*, by Richard Lavoie

*Beyond F.A.T. City: A Look Back, A Look Ahead Disabilities*, by Richard Lavoie

*The Motivation Breakthrough: 6 Secrets to Turning On the Tuned-Out Child*, by Richard Lavoie

*ADD & Loving It?!* with Patrick McKenna (Primary Contributor) and Rick Green (Director)

## The most interesting book I ever read:

*Animals in Translation: Using the Mysteries of Autism to Decode Animal Behavior*, by Temple Grandin and Catherine Johnson

## ABOUT THE AUTHOR

Dr. Tavares is physician in Manitoba, Canada. He works for Prairie Mountain Health in Western Manitoba. Dr. Tavares recently started writing, in his after-work hours, essays on patient safety and on the experiences of children and teenagers growing up with poor attention or different learning styles. Dr. Tavares is a strong believer in the power of patient- and family-centred care positively transforming the medical system.

## Other Titles by Alexandre Tavares

*On Board with Your Treatment! For a Safe Treatment Every Time!*

# TERMS OF USE AGREEMENT

This writer was advised to include this statement at the end of this book.

Dr. Tavares

**Acceptance**

It is important that you read all the following terms and conditions carefully.

This Terms of Use Agreement ("Agreement") is a legal agreement between you and Dr. Alexandre Garcia Tavares ("Dr. Tavares"), the copyright owner ("Owner") of this book, *Super Heroes Do Exist!* How a Physician Came to Believe in Teachers who are True Super Heroes (the "book Super Heroes Do Exist"). It states the terms and conditions under which you may use the book *Super Heroes Do Exist* and other materials displayed or made available through the book *Super Heroes Do Exist*, including, without limitation, articles, text, photographs, images, illustrations, audio clips, video clips. By accessing and using the book *Super Heroes Do Exist*, you are indicating your acceptance to be bound by the terms and conditions of this Agreement. If you do not accept these terms and conditions, you must not use the book.

**Medical emergency**

Do not use the book *Super Heroes Do Exist* for medical emergencies. If you have a medical emergency, call a physician or qualified health-care provider, or call 911 immediately. Under no circumstances should you attempt self-treatment based on anything you have seen or read in the book *Super Heroes Do Exist*.

**General information not medical advice**

The general information provided in the book *Super Heroes Do Exist* is for informational purposes only and is not professional medical advice, diagnosis, treatment, or care, nor is it intended to be a substitute therefore.

Always seek the advice of your physician or other qualified health provider properly licensed to practice medicine or general health care in your jurisdiction concerning any questions you may have regarding any information obtained from the book *Super Heroes Do Exist* and any medical condition you believe may be relevant to you or to someone else. Never disregard professional medical advice or delay in seeking it because of something you have read on the book *Super Heroes Do Exist*. Always consult with your physician or other qualified health-care provider before embarking on a new treatment, diet, or fitness program. Information obtained in the book *Super Heroes Do Exist* is not exhaustive and does not cover all diseases, ailments, physical conditions, or their treatment.

### No physician-patient relationship
The presentation of general information in the book *Super Heroes Do Exist* does not establish a physician-patient relationship between you and Dr. Tavares and is not intended as a solicitation of individuals to become patients or clients of Dr. Tavares.

### No endorsements
Unless specifically stated, Dr. Tavares does not recommend or endorse any specific brand of products, services, or procedures.

### E-mail communication with the public
Dr. Tavares does not wish to use this book as a means of communication with the public (i) regarding questions or issues of a medical nature; (ii) to establish physician-patient relationships; (iii) to book or cancel appointments; or (iv) for enquiries regarding fees, services, or similar matters. E-mail communications regarding such matters will not be responded to and will be discarded unread.

### Disclaimer of warranties
The book *Super Heroes Do Exist* and the content are provided "as is" and "as available." While Dr. Tavares endeavours to provide information that is correct, accurate, current, and timely, Dr. Tavares makes no representations, warranties, or covenants, express or implied, regarding the book *Super Heroes Do Exist* and the content including, without limitation, no representation, warranty, or covenant (i) that the content contained in or made available through the book *Super Heroes Do Exist* or any item(s) made available on or through the book *Super Heroes Do Exist* will be of merchantable quality and/or fit for a particular purpose; (ii) that the book *Super Heroes Do Exist* or content will be accurate, complete, current, reliable, timely, or suitable for any particular purpose; (iii) that the operation of the book *Super Heroes Do Exist* will be uninterrupted or error-free; (iv) that defects or errors in the book *Super Heroes Do Exist* or the content, be it human or computer errors, will be corrected; (v) that the book *Super Heroes Do Exist* will be free from viruses or harmful components; and (vi) that communications to or from your e-book reader will be secure and/or not intercepted.

You acknowledge and agree that your access to and use of the book *Super Heroes Do Exist* and the content is entirely at your own risk and liability.

### Limitation of liability

In no event shall Dr. Tavares, officers, directors, employees, agents, licensors, and their respective successors and assignees be liable for damages of any kind, including, without limitation, any direct, special, indirect, punitive, incidental, or consequential damages including, without limitation, any loss or damages in the nature of, or relating to, lost business, medical injury, personal injury, wrongful death, improper diagnosis, inaccurate information, improper treatment, or any other loss incurred in connection with your use, misuse, or reliance upon the book *Super Heroes Do Exist* or the content, or your inability to use the book *Super Heroes Do Exist*, regardless of the cause and whether arising in contract (including fundamental breach), tort (including negligence), or otherwise. The foregoing limitation shall apply even if Dr. Tavares knew of or ought to have known of the possibility of such damages.

Dr. Tavares also expressly disclaims any and all liability for the acts, omissions, and conduct of any third-party user of the book *Super Heroes Do Exist*, or any advertiser or sponsor of the book *Super Heroes Do Exist* ("third-party"). Under no circumstances shall Dr. Tavares, officers, directors, employees, agents, licensors, and their respective successors and assigns be liable for any injury, loss, damage (including direct, special, indirect, punitive, incidental, or consequential damages), or expense arising in any manner whatsoever from (i) the acts, omissions, or conduct of any third-party; and (ii) any access, use, reliance upon, or inability to use any materials, content, goods, or services located at, or made available at, any website linked to or from the book *Super Heroes Do Exist*, regardless of the cause and whether arising in contract (including fundamental breach), tort (including negligence), or otherwise. The foregoing limitation shall apply even if Dr. Tavares knew of or ought to have known of the possibility of such damages.

**Indemnity**

You agree to indemnify, defend, and hold harmless Dr. Tavares and its officers, directors, employees, agents, licensors, and their respective successors and assignees, from and against any and all claims, demands, liabilities, costs, or expenses whatsoever, including, without limitation, legal fees and disbursements, resulting directly or indirectly from (i) your breach of any of the terms and conditions of this Agreement; (ii) your access to, use, misuse, reliance upon, or inability to access or use the book *Super Heroes Do Exist*, the content, or any website to which the book *Super Heroes Do Exist* is or may be linked to from time to time or; (iii) your use of, reliance on, publication, communication, distribution, uploading, or downloading of anything (including the content) on or from the book *Super Heroes Do Exist*.

## Copyright

The content of the book *Super Heroes Do Exist* is protected by copyright law and is owned by Dr. Tavares. Except as granted in the limited licence herein, any use of the content, including modification, transmission, presentation, distribution, republication, or other exploitation of the book *Super Heroes Do Exist* or of its content, whether in whole or in part, is prohibited without the express prior written consent of Dr. Tavares.

Dr. Tavares created and edited this book in almost complete entirety (about 98 percent of it) outside his regular working hours, so his employer agreed Dr. Tavares is the legitimate sole copyright holder of this book and also the sole copyright holder of the book "On Board with Your Treatment! For a Safe Treatment Every Time!"

## Limited licence

Subject to the terms and conditions of this Agreement, you are hereby granted a limited, nontransferable, and non-exclusive licence to access, view, and use the book *Super Heroes Do Exist* and the content for your personal, noncommercial use. You should maintain all copyright and other notices contained in such content. You may not copy and/or repost items comprising the content online. You must also abide by any additional requirements governing the use of any specific content that may be set out in the book *Super Heroes Do Exist*. In the event of a conflict between the terms of a licence governing specific content and this Agreement, the terms of the specific licence shall govern.

## Linking

The book *Super Heroes Do Exist* contains links to third-party websites. These links are provided solely as a convenience to you and not as an endorsement by Dr. Tavares of any third-party website or the content thereof. Unless expressly stated, Dr. Tavares does not operate any third-party website linked to the book *Super Heroes Do Exist* and is not responsible for the content of any third-party website, nor does it make any representation, warranty, or covenant of any kind regarding any third-party Website including, without limitation, (i) any representation, warranty, or covenant regarding the legality, accuracy, reliability, completeness, timeliness, or suitability of any content on such third-party websites; (ii) any representation, warranty, or covenant regarding the merchantability and/or fitness for a particular purpose of any third-party websites or material, content, software, goods, or services located at or made available through such third-party websites; or (iii) any representation, warranty, or covenant that the operation of such third-party websites will be uninterrupted or error free, that defects or errors in such third-party websites will be corrected, or that such third-party websites will be free from viruses or other harmful components.

While Dr. Tavares included links to websites in the book *Super Heroes Do Exist*, the book *Super Heroes Do Exist* should not wish to be linked to or from any third-party website which contains, posts, or transmits any unlawful or indecent information of any kind, including, without limitation (i) any content constituting or encouraging conduct that would constitute a criminal offence, give rise to civil liability, or otherwise violate any local, state, provincial, territorial, national, international law or regulation which may be damaging or detrimental to the activities, operations, credibility, or integrity of Dr. Tavares; or (ii) any website which contains, posts, or transmits any material or information of any kind which violates or infringes upon the rights of others, including material which is an invasion of privacy or publicity rights, or which is protected by copyright, trademark, or other proprietary rights. Dr. Tavares reserves the right to prohibit or refuse to accept any link to the book

*Super Heroes Do Exist*, including, without limitation, any link which contains or makes available any content or information of the foregoing nature, at any time. You agree to remove any link you may have to the book *Super Heroes Do Exist* upon the request of Dr. Tavares.

**Submissions**

The Amazon website and external websites may provide features which allow you to post messages and book reviews of the book *Super Heroes Do Exist*. Dr. Tavares does not control the content of any submissions and has no obligation to monitor the submissions. However, Dr. Tavares reserves the right at all times to disclose any information necessary to satisfy any law, regulation, or governmental or law-enforcement request.

You acknowledge that you alone are responsible for the content of your submissions and the consequences thereof.

**Tools**

Any tools or calculators provided in the book *Super Heroes Do Exist* are provided for general and illustrative purposes only.

Such tools and/or calculators are not medical advice nor are they intended to be a substitute therefore.

You should not act or abstain from acting based on any information provided by any such tool or calculator available on this book.

**Security**

Any information sent or received over the Internet is generally not secure. Dr. Tavares cannot guarantee the security or confidentiality of any communication using the Internet.

### Modification to Book

Dr. Tavares reserves the right any time, and from time to time, to modify or not publish anymore, temporarily or permanently, the book *Super Heroes Do Exist*, and make the new versions available or not. Dr. Tavares shall have no liability to you or any third party for any modifications, suspension, or withdrawal of the publication of the book *Super Heroes Do Exist* or any part thereof.

### Use prohibited where contrary to law

Use of this book is unauthorized in any jurisdiction where the book *Super Heroes Do Exist* or any of the content may violate any laws or regulations. You agree not to access or use the book *Super Heroes Do Exist* in such jurisdictions. You agree that you are responsible for compliance with all applicable laws or regulations. Any contravention of this provision (or any provision of this Agreement) is entirely at your own risk.

### Governing law and jurisdiction

The book *Super Heroes Do Exist* was written by Dr. Tavares from his offices within the province of Manitoba, Canada. Dr. Tavares is licensed by the College of Physicians and Surgeons of Manitoba to practice medicine in province of Manitoba, Canada. You agree that all matters relating to your access or use of the book *Super Heroes Do Exist* and its content shall be governed by the laws of the province or territory of Manitoba, Canada, and the laws of Canada applicable therein, without regard to conflict of laws principles. You agree and hereby submit to the exclusive and preferential jurisdiction of the courts of the province of Manitoba with respect to all matters relating to your access and use of the book *Super Heroes Do Exist* and the content as well as any dispute that may arise therefrom and that the applicable law shall be the law of the province of Manitoba and of Canada.

### Waiver

Any consent by Dr. Tavares to, or waiver of, a breach of this Agreement which you have committed, whether express or implied, shall not constitute a consent to, or waiver of any other, different or subsequent breach.

### Severability

The invalidity or unenforceability of any provision of this Agreement or any covenant contained herein shall not affect the validity or enforceability of any other provision or covenant contained herein and any such invalid provision or covenant shall be deemed severable from the rest of this

Agreement.

**Entire Agreement**

This is the entire Agreement between you and Dr. Tavares relating to your access and use of the book *Super Heroes Do Exist*.

Made in the USA
Middletown, DE
11 October 2018